ALL ABOARD THE SHAPES TRAIN

Illustrated by

sean sims

STATION

OXFORD

UNIVERSITY PRESS

We're at the station. We're off to explore playtime **shapes** and so much more.

All aboard!

There are **circles** everywhere!

The bubbles, balls and
bugs are circles.

The adventure castle is made up of lots of **squares**.

Toot toot!
Where will the train take us next?

Lots of **triangles** at the lake!

Butterflies, boats and trees.

We can make a robot out of **rectangles!**

Time for a snack at the café.
Look at all the **diamonds!**

Now we are flying our kites!

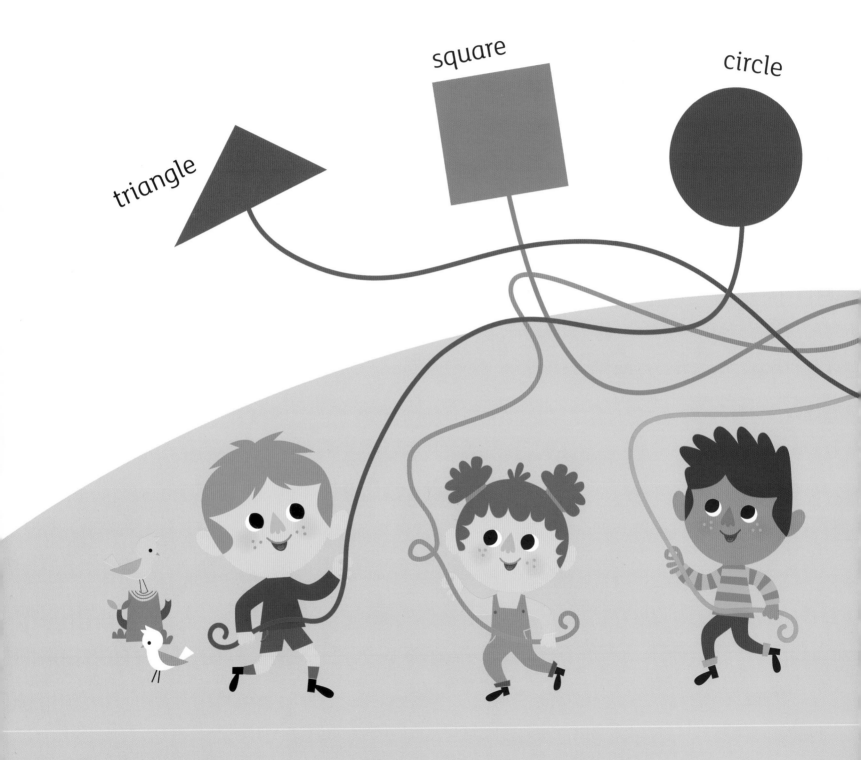

triangle

square

circle

Who does each shape belong to?

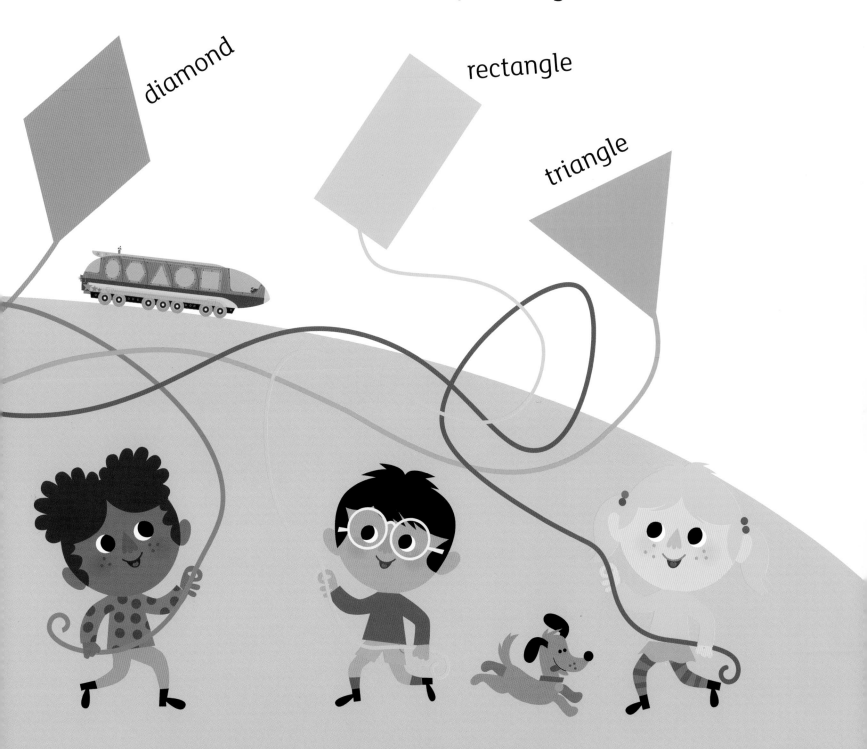

diamond

rectangle

triangle

Playtime is always full of shapes.
What **shapes** can you see here?

We're playing with even more shapes!

semi-circles

ovals

Here are **hexagons, pentagons, semi-circles** and **ovals!**

pentagons

hexagons

Wow! We're travelling through the fairground!

All these **patterns** are made from shapes.

We're watching fireworks at the fairground . . .

. . . the sky is bursting with **spirals** and **stars!**

Can you remember all the shapes
we saw on the journey?

It's time to go home.

All aboard!

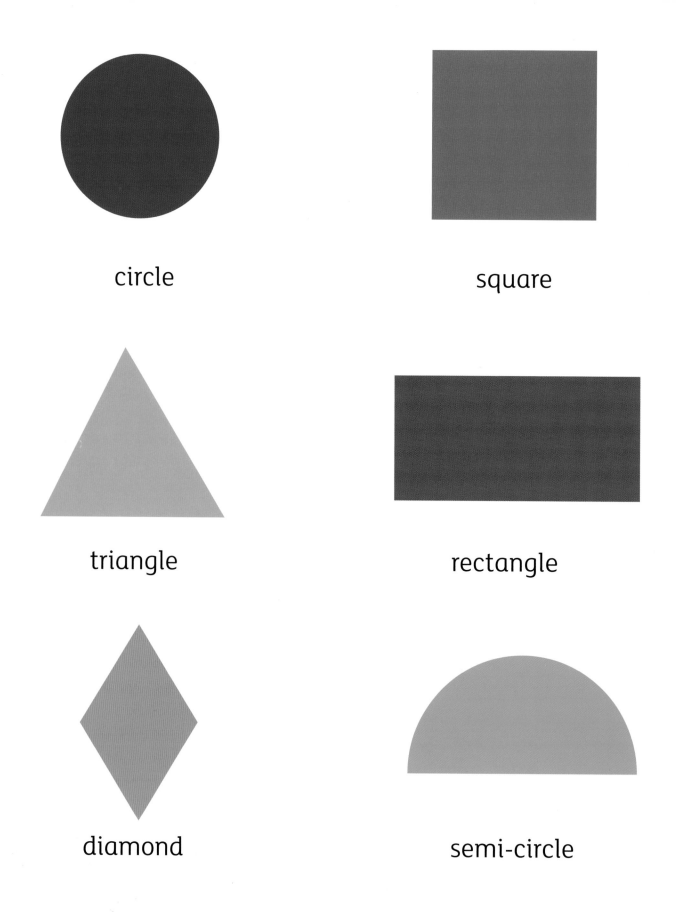

circle

square

triangle

rectangle

diamond

semi-circle

oval

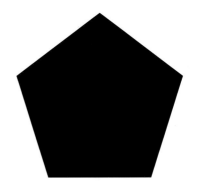

pentagon

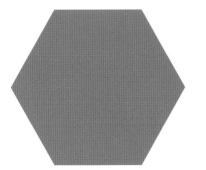

hexagon

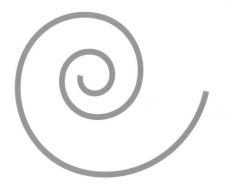

spiral

star

OXFORD

UNIVERSITY PRESS

Great Clarendon Street, Oxford OX2 6DP

Oxford University Press is a department of the University of Oxford.
It furthers the University's objective of excellence in research, scholarship,
and education by publishing worldwide. Oxford is a registered trade mark
of Oxford University Press in the UK and in certain other countries

British Library Cataloguing in Publication Data

Data available

ISBN: 978-0-19277472-9

1 3 5 7 9 10 8 6 4 2

Printed in China

Paper used in the production of this book is a natural,
recyclable product made from wood grown in sustainable forests.
The manufacturing process conforms to the environmental
regulations of the country of origin.